(Theresa McD) 7 50

D1228885

゠゠゠゠゠゠゠゠゠゠゠゠゠゠゠゠゠゠゠゠゠゠゠゠゠゠゠゠゠゠゠゠゠゠゠゠

THE INC
ISHMENT OF THE

゠゠゠゠゠゠゠゠゠゠゠゠゠゠゠゠゠゠゠゠゠゠゠゠゠゠゠゠゠゠゠゠゠゠゠゠

THE
UNIVERSITY OF WINNIPEG
PORTAGE & BALMORAL
WINNIPEG 2. MAN.   CANADA

DISCARDED

GREEN FIELDS AFAR

Ct
310
.M5A3

GREEN FIELDS AFAR

MEMORIES OF ALBERTA DAYS

CLARA and J. E. MIDDLETON

Drawings by Thoreau MacDonald

THE RYERSON PRESS

TORONTO   HALIFAX   VANCOUVER

COPYRIGHT, CANADA, 1947, BY
THE RYERSON PRESS, TORONTO

All rights reserved. No part of this book may be repro-
duced in any form (except by reviewers for the public
press), without permission in writing from the publishers.

Published November, 1947

PRINTED AND BOUND IN CANADA
BY THE RYERSON PRESS, TORONTO

Foreword

TALKING about one's first husband to one's second husband is supposed to be both difficult and unwise; I have not found it so. They two were boyhood friends and brothers-in-law, singing together in the country choir, playing in the country band; the one blatting fearsomely on the E Flat Bass horn, the other trilling on the second B Flat cornet. They had fun together and, while both lived, mutual admiration.

So while I knitted and talked before our fireplace in 1947 my husband seemed uncommonly attentive and when each talk faded out he was likely to make a furtive excursion to his typewriter in the library. One day he laid before me this record of my chatter.

He is said to be a journalist, but prefers to call himself a reporter. I fancy he has always been a good one, for this story is so accurate an echo of my talk that it startled me. The only thing I missed in it were the ragged edges and lumpy bits common to ordinary conversation.

So here is my small adventure in living, which we like to think is a type of the universal activity, diligence and ambition that helped to create a nation.

C. J. M.

I

I HAD been tired, tired; not for days only but for months. Now, coming into Calgary after an unbroken journey of eight hundred miles, I was feeling somewhat rested, a fact that didn't make sense to me at the time. Later I learned that people living at four thousand feet above the sea, or thereabouts, were of two sorts; those who wilted and those who were stimulated. The thin, lively air and the sunshine gave me a perpetual lift; and do even yet.

We stepped off the train before a small frame station like hundreds of others along the railroad line; as if Calgary were a dull hamlet instead of a bustling cow-town seeing itself almost a metropolis. It was July, 1904. A bench ran all about the station and at one corner sat a well-rounded squaw displaying baskets and bead-work for sale. A few Indians, doing nothing,

1

but without enthusiasm, leaned against the station and for the first time I saw cowboys, half a dozen of them, each costumed according to rule; high-heeled boots with spurs, "chaps," a dingy flannel shirt, a neckerchief, red or blue, and an enormous felt hat. The rest of the people in and about the station, were just as ordinary as we were, though I noticed several measuring with their eyes the height and breadth of my good husband.

We crossed Ninth Avenue, which had a wooden sidewalk, found a modest hotel—I think, the Commercial House—and got settled. Then my husband went out to find a first cousin of his. The Englishes had long been spotted about London Township, Ontario, like raisins in a good cake. Now they were flavouring Western Canada as well. Representatives of the family were in Winnipeg, Portage La Prairie and Virden, while in Calgary Tom English was Chief of Police, knowing everybody and universally known.

He was big and straight in his blue tunic with brass buttons, but there was no "uniform" quality in his broad-brimmed grey felt hat; a cross in hats between the Mountie's Stetson and the cowboy's "ten-gallon." His hospitality was generous and genuine. If his wife had been at home, he explained, instead of at Portage with their daughter Maud—but daughter Bess would look after us. A hotel? Not to be heard of! Soon Mrs. Tomlinson arrived and shepherded us to her pleasant apartment on Eighth Avenue over a store.

That evening two young friends of the Tomlinsons dropped in; Kenny McEwen and Russell Elliott, the former a railway employee, the latter a distant kinsman of mine who was just entering on a new job, as a clerk in the City Hall. In telling them about my brother-in-law Free, in his private freight car, with four milch cows, six horses, a crate of chickens and our household goods, I spoke of the mighty lunch I had put up for him, and said that he would wash it down with milk.

2

Mr. McEwen looked serious. "If he drinks milk from cows in transit I'm afraid he'll be sick. When do you expect the car to arrive?"

We explained that we were supposed to be two or three days ahead of it.

"You never know about freight," was the reply. "What does your brother look like?"

"Six feet tall, thick-set and in dark grey clothes."

"With a black soft felt hat?" We nodded. "That car went on to Carstairs this morning. It was only a short time in the yard."

Clearly, my husband must go north by the next train and I would stay in Calgary for a week to send up food supplies, to await the building of a shelter of some sort and the setting up of a stove and enough furniture for a bit of housekeeping in the raw. That week was a month long, despite the gracious Tomlinsons.

But the day of departure came at last and when my train climbed the side of the big saucer in which Calgary sits I got a noble view of the mountains. I found it hard to believe that they were seventy miles away. I could have accepted seven miles, perhaps fifteen, but not seventy, so clear was the outline of the peaks.

Carstairs had a station; a box car without wheels set down beside the track. And there was my Homer with a team and the democrat. But he looked a bit "streaked."

"You'll have to stay here a few days," he said. "We've been too sick to work. There's no house, not even a shack. We're sleeping in a tent."

"If you're sleeping in a tent," I replied, "so can I. And I won't stay here a minute without you." I was steadfast, immovable, like the mountains, and Homer gave up the argument before it had really got started.

He told me that a neighbour's boy had come four miles to bring the tent and help put it up. He had opened a can of

3

salmon for supper, leaving it in the can—in sunlight. That night he had nearly died, and both Free and Homer had been affected, though not so seriously. Free, as we had feared, had been ill on the train, and this new attack took the starch out of him. It was apparent that I was needed to manage affairs and feed those boys properly. So after a dull meal in a dull and fly-infested hotel I climbed into the democrat which was well-loaded with bits of our furniture and Homer click-clicked to the horses.

In a minute or less we were out of Carstairs on a well-marked trail and headed east on a jaunt of eighteen miles. I noticed with delight that the prairie was not as dead-flat as in Saskatchewan or North Dakota. The grasses were lush and knee-high; gaillardia and wild roses were flourishing and frequently a little lake, or slough, appeared, dotted with wild duck. Off in the distance cattle herds were grazing and we saw several prairie chicken whirling up from the grass.

We passed three or four homesteaders' shacks but saw nobody, and after six miles or so came to the edge of the Rosebud Creek coulée. I was startled. Here was a valley sixty feet below us and perhaps a half-mile wide, the bed of some ancient river. The banks were steep. To go straight down would have been easy enough on horseback, but for a loaded wagon the trail eased itself down in a winding course. Even then it was somewhat alarming to a stranger. The creek was not deep and we forded it without difficulty and took a slanting way to the top of the opposite bank.

From that point onward there were no roads or settled trails. We set our course due east across the open prairie, following the dim track our own wagon had made day after day in bringing out our belongings. In time we came to another slashed-out river bed, Sheep coulée, not as fearsome as the Rosebud, forded its small brook and had only some six miles to go.

4

Homer was telling me some of the oddities of arriving nowhere and calling it home. He mentioned the obvious surprise of the cows and horses, accustomed to stacks and stables. He laughed about the chickens. As they were let out of the crate which had confined them for a week they walked stiff-legged here and there, pausing to pick up a grasshopper, or to investigate some strange plant with seeds ready for the picking. They seemed ill at ease, especially as daylight was fading. At last, with a "what's the use" expression they went back into the crate for rest and shelter.

He told me of the first big load brought out in the lumber wagon; several packing cases marked for earliest opening, since they contained bedding or cooking utensils, a large steel range, the pride of my heart, and a hundredweight of coal. Both at the Rosebud and at Sheep coulée the load had to be lightened, and two trips were necessary. It was past sunset and obviously, the horses at a slow walking gait would not be able to finish the journey before dark. It was hard enough to keep direction in daylight. To follow the dim trail at night would be impossible. So the load was dumped on the prairie, steel range and all, and the team at a brisk trot reached the tent in early twilight. Next morning the boys went back for the load.

I remember thinking, home was never like this, yet I was not depressed. The week of worry and waiting was over. The boys were well again, the air was fresh and sweet, we had 160 acres of good land which would grow anything, and we knew how to work—and like it. So it was in a surge of cheerfulness that I saw beyond a shining slough a tent set on a rise above a little creek bed.

While the boys were unhitching I made an inspection. Here was a bell tent, such as the soldiers at home used on Carling Heights, supposed to accommodate eight men, at a pinch. The range had been put up, half in and half out, with the pipe sticking up crazily and far enough away from the canvas. A double-bed mattress was supported on a rough

5

frame of two-by-fours and our red couch stood about two feet from it, on the other side of the main pole. I dragged a piece of carpet out of one of the packing cases and pinned it up, separating the bed and the couch. So we had a two-room apartment, suitable for any married couple, with an understanding brother-in-law. And there we slept the sleep of the just and the weary while awaiting the building of a proper house. And the blessed sun shone every day.

II

SINCE four boys and three girls made up the Russell family in
London, Ontario, I am not surprised that there was some con-
fusion about my birthday. Father held that December 16th
was the date. Mother, who possibly had a more personal
interest, stood out for the 15th. Whatever the date, I was
born; of a Russell-Wheaton ancestry; Scottish-Irish in blood
and farming pioneers in the Township of London.

Rheumatism drove my father off the land to a coal-and-wood
business in London when that city was little more than a county
town. Firewood of beech and maple was a regular winter crop
on the farms around. Father bought it in quantity, used a
steam power-saw to cut it to sixteen-inch length, and sold it,
delivered, at from five to six dollars a cord. Not until the bush-
lands began to thin out and the general price of cordwood rose

was there much popular interest in coal for domestic uses, even though the best Pennsylvania anthracite was available in London at seven dollars a ton.

I remember when the big wood stove in our front hall was replaced by an imposing base-burner with little mica windows all about and a knight in armour on the top. Clearly the coal-and-wood business sixty years ago was not an easy way of getting rich. I have no notion of Father's annual profits, save that they were not large. But, with carefulness, they were adequate. Food of the best quality was cheap. Plain clothes were not too dear, when made at home, and hay and oats for our horse came at low cost from country relations and friends.

In addition to our base-burner we had a wood stove in the living room, a smaller one, for state occasions, in the parlour, and a big kitchen range. The pipes went through the ceiling, and one swelled out into a heating-drum in the upstairs hall. The bedrooms, in cold weather, helped to train us in speedy dressing and undressing. And if the water in the ewer were frozen one could always wash in the kitchen. There was no running water and our "powder-room" was a small building at the back of the yard near the stable.

Not until I was, perhaps, twelve years old did the city provide a water and sewer system of proper size and compel residents on the principal streets to make use of it. Our well was a good one, and convenient to the back door. I seem to remember murmurings at taking water from rusty old pipes instead of from a cool, clear spring-well and a wooden pump.

Our house, of white brick, was as big as the family; even bigger, for it had nine bedrooms, a mighty dining-room, an unused parlour and a kitchen, large and inconvenient. Its pine floor had to be scrubbed periodically on hands and knees and its great range had to be polished after the similitude of a palace. The other rooms were carpeted, some of Brussels, but mostly of rags, wound by the children into balls and woven "hit-and-miss" by a neighbour with a loom. Friday was sweep-

8

ing day and those carpets were reluctant in yielding dust to the broom, so the shoulder muscles of the sweeper were built-up.

Monday was wash-day and for some years my mother had the regular aid of a coloured woman who charged thirty-five cents a day. She had two meals with us, but that didn't count. No one figured on the cost of food. That would have been thought small and mean. The food was there, to be eaten— and welcome. There had been a financial panic in 1873 and the depression had lasted long. For years a good man's wages at the yard stayed at a dollar a day. Naturally, in the ideas of the times, a woman was worth not half as much as a man. I remember that when the "washwoman" raised her price to fifty cents Mother looked appraisingly at me, the eldest daughter, and said, "We'll do it ourselves."

She was slender, dark-haired, wiry, beneath her smooth and rosy skin and as resolute and vivid as she was lovely. Generally there was a baby in her arms. One night I heard "doings" below stairs, and came down in my nightgown to find a new brother being washed—and protesting. "Go back to bed," Mother said. "You may see him in the morning."

Before going to school and after getting home each of the children had some specified work to do. Beds had to be made, rooms had to be dusted, ironing had to be done, the garden had to be weeded, wood had to be brought in, potatoes had to be peeled; chores and errands multiplied. On Saturday nights boots had to be cleaned and frilled petticoats ironed, and the girls' hair washed and curled in preparation for service at First Presbyterian Church, many long blocks away. My brothers, each in his turn, had a morning paper route which got them out of bed at five o'clock, so, all in all, there was but little time for play. Yet it was a happy home, with no juvenile delinquents.

So the years wore away. My eldest brother was employed by a wholesale drug house, and came home from an out-of-town trip with typhoid fever. It was in 1888, the time of the first

9

influenza visitation. Hospitals were crowded, doctors were run ragged, nurses and maids were unobtainable. I nursed him through three terrible months and when at last he was able to sit up I drew his rocking chair one morning to the front window where he watched the pallbearers carrying mother to the hearse. Toil, anxiety and influenza had been too much for her brave and loving heart.

I was sixteen years old, a milliner's apprentice, going down town every day. But the family had to be mothered and fed, and my father, weary and broken, had no taste for a stranger in the house. He turned in confidence to me and for ten years housekeeping was my task. But I was healthy and strong, and the atmosphere of affection and co-operation was stimulating. One by one the boys married and left. When I found my good man and went home with him only my father and two sisters were left in a house with nine bedrooms and acres of rag carpet. Naturally as housekeeper I had been busy. But I had some leisure, took a few piano lessons, sang in the church choir and made many friends.

During the American Civil War wheat prices had been high and a considerable prosperity followed. Throughout the townships about London large brick houses and good barns became the rule rather than the exception. Grandfather Wheaton's place on the Third Concession of London Township was imposing in our eyes and we welcomed every opportunity to go visiting there. So also at an uncle's. And going up to Kennedys' was always an occasion, for Mrs. Hal. Kennedy had been my mother's bridesmaid and the Russell children were received there almost as nephews and nieces. Eleven miles north of London was a long journey; two hours at least in the buggy, longer in democrat or lumber wagon, but we travelled hopefully and arrived with joy.

For where else could be found such a happy family with Hal. leading the laughter? Where else such thick cream, such a pitcher of maple syrup continually on the table, such an

10

orchard full of fine apples, such a swing in the big spruces enclosing the front lawn, and such a deep shade in the woods, to be explored in company with Bert, Minnie and Margaret, the Kennedy children of our own age?

As I grew older the Patterson home was inviting; still farther north—almost to Denfield, *ultima thule* to us. For Cicely and the boys were musically-minded and sang to admiration. Also they were high-spirited and gay, known and beloved for miles around. So many were our friends in the country that we never followed the small-city custom of regarding farm-folk as an inferior order of humanity. I, at least, always had the country mind and preferred a country party or a country dance to any entertainment the city could provide. The snobbery of some dry goods clerk or bank teller, out for the evening in a dress suit, was not so pleasant as the natural talk and laughter of young farmers who could plow all day and dance all night without turning a hair. So it was no social wrench for me to marry such a farmer; Homer Jackson, six feet, four inches tall, proportionately broad, whose humour was perennial, and whose talk was starry with wit.

For all my Homer's fine social qualities, which made him popular in any company, he was shy at bottom, and positively trembled at the thought of "a big wedding." So he arranged with Rev. Dr. Clark to have the ceremony in the church on a Wednesday evening before prayer-meeting. Nobody was invited, but the news leaked out—probably through Cicely Patterson, my bridesmaid—and we got hints that a congregation was in the making. Homer sought out Dr. Clark again and had the ceremony advanced half an hour. As we left the church we saw people coming from various directions—all too late.

Low prices and small acreage had no great future for a young couple starting out in the world and my husband grew restless. His elder brother Freeman had gone west and found a moderate prosperity in North Dakota. That year Free came home for Christmas and had a suggestion. He had left his farm and moved to Grand Forks to give his boys a chance to go to college while he applied himself to carpentry and general building. Perhaps, he thought, Brother Homer would like to join him, working with him in the winter, and taking over the farm in the following spring.

I had no urge to go adventuring but since Homer was bent on it that was enough for me. So we journeyed westward taking with us two orphaned nephews, aged 18 and 15. In a late April we left Grand Forks for the prairie farm and found the little house almost buried in snow.

In all the three years that we spent in North Dakota the kindness of the neighbours was not sufficient to balance the cruelty of the climate. And besides ill-fortune dogged us. We lost our baby son. The summer heat brought to life a million bedbugs, the heritage left by a "renter" who had taken the farm when Free left it and had stayed until our arrival. And to crown it all I came home, after a brief visit east, to find one of the nephews seriously ill of *smallpox!* The elder had had it lightly, thinking it measles or chicken-pox, and so nursed his brother in the granary while I washed and fumigated, disinfected and washed for two solid months.

North Dakota, no doubt, is a pleasant State, for those who like it. For us, within three years, it had become a howling wilderness, a sort of purgatory which, we feared, would go on forever and ever. Then word came—from somewhere—that ranch lands in Western Canada, near Calgary, were being opened for settlement. My husband looked once at me, and I at him. It was autumn, and the crop was in. Homer, our nephew Bert, and a friend entrained for Calgary. They found that the land available was about twenty miles east of Carstairs. A prospective settler could file on the quarter-section of his choice and after performing the usual settlement duties could pre-empt another quarter at a nominal charge per acre. A government agent drove the men out from Carstairs; gave them their choice of location. Homer made his title clear and came back to me with shining eyes. It was good land, in a good climate, and we would move in the following spring.

But the winter was a savage one and Homer got pneumonia. It was a serious case. Free came out to the farm to help me and we brought him safely through. But he was not strong enough to go travelling until July. Even then Free determined to come with us and help build our house. He and our nephews loaded on a freight car our horses and chickens, furniture and gear, and he alone went with it to Carstairs. Some days later Homer and I were driven north across the International boundary to Crystal City, Manitoba, went to Winnipeg for a brief stay with old friends and then set out for Calgary.

Some say that the prairie is dreary and monotonous. Not for me. I had sheer delight to see it sliding past the car window. Difficulties and troubles might lie ahead, hardships might come, but to my weary mind any change was for the better. We had had many good neighbours in North Dakota but they all had seemed to hold the opinion that the United States was God's country, that all others were beneath consideration and that the poor slaves inhabiting them were in the darkness of barbarism.

A minor source of irritation, no doubt! I should have smiled. But to me it was a thorn in the flesh, a messenger of Satan to buffet me. Now I was to be free and perhaps, before long, I might see a Union Jack. I looked long without success. Canadians do not flaunt their colours as a rule, save on special occasions. But at last, in a Manitoba school yard, I saw it flapping in the wind until it was dimmed by the moisture in my eyes. Before the day was done I saw another brave sight, a constable of the Mounted Police in the King's scarlet, watching the train go by.

III

BEFORE digging the cellar for our fine new house we had to
make sure that it would be on our property. All we knew was
that a bit north and west of our tent, and across the creek-bed,
was the corner stake, a sturdy bit of iron anchored in cement,
but almost concealed by the grass. We had to find the other
three stakes of the half-mile square enclosing our acres.

The official description said something about "forty chains
more or less east from the northwest corner," and so on. We
had no compass and no long measuring tape, but we knew that
the hind wheels of our democrat were *so* high—I forget the exact
figure—and we had a general idea that east was where the sun
rose. So on the Sunday following my arrival we hitched up
and climbed into the chariot. Free had tied a white rag on
one of the hind wheel spokes; my task was to count the

14

revolutions while Homer drove eastward. When my count passed two hundred the boys got out and in a few minutes found the stake. Following the same procedure we gradually bounded our quarter-section and found it very good. The house-site was certainly on the estate.

We knew that a road allowance was on one side of our place and assumed that it would be on the north. So the house would face that way, for convenience in watching the people drive by—when there would be people. The cellar was dug, 24 by 18 feet, the general plan being not on a blueprint but in our heads. For the present a clay floor for the cellar would have to do.

Large stones were brought up from the creek-bed as corner foundations and midway supports, and then, with four-by-fours nine inches apart, we laid the beginning of our walls. The space between was packed tight with clay until we came to ground level. From there onwards the task was not difficult. Soon the upright studdings were in place, with a four-by-four stringer, and while Homer and I nailed on the rough outside sheeting Free was cutting and raising rafters.

Then came shingling time. Homer was never any good on a roof, or a stack, or any elevation. Ladders were deadly threats, so far as he was concerned. They made him giddy. So while he kept his feet on the ground and his hands busy at ground tasks I went on the roof with Free and helped him lay and nail six or seven "squares" of shingles. I wore a sweater, an old skirt and a flannel petticoat, for in those days no woman of taste would have been seen in men's pants or overalls. There was a time, a little later, when I had a divided skirt for riding, but even that seemed a little less than modest and decent.

Soon we had a roof over our heads and could afford to let Free go home. Doors for front and back, and window frames already glazed, we brought out from Carstairs and set in place. We even had two screen doors which were put on before the clapboarding was on the sides. The rough sheeting, of course,

15

was not tight and there was justice in the comment of our first caller, an elderly and lean cynic from Missouri. He shifted his cud and said, "This here's quite a house. Cracks in the walls to let the flies in and screen doors to keep 'em from gittin' out."

There was not time for frills in building, such as clapboarding and inside sheeting. The summer was wearing on and we had to put up hay for our present stock and for the cattle we hoped to get. So building halted for a while in face of that emergency.

The downstairs was one big room, but I made it look like two by putting up a pair of chenille curtains on cranes from the side walls. So we had a living-room, a dining-room and kitchen combined, and a pantry under the staircase. The range gleamed bright. The extension table, the sideboard and the kitchen cabinet were in place. The red couch, a writing desk and two easy chairs looked well in the living-room and I had gay curtains on the windows. But the walls were still bare; rough studding and open cracks. I got a roll of grey building paper and a bunch of dressed lath. In a couple of days I had rooms smart enough for anybody. The soft colour of the paper when stretched tight was easy to look at and made a good background for our furniture. And the flies couldn't get in.

The upstairs was partitioned to make two rooms. Our two good bedroom sets, complete with bureaux, wash-stands, pitchers, etc., were in place, and in the larger room we put up an extra bed. So we were all prepared for company as soon as company might come.

After the house was built we learned that the road allowance was on the west front, rather than on the north. When our private trail from the road was made, the approach was to our back door, which was most improper. Also, for lack of a compass, the house did not bear directly north-and-south. Viewed from the road it had, on its little eminence, a distinctly cock-eyed appearance, though not an uncheerful one. It was a good house. We thanked God for it and took courage while going on with the haying, Homer on the mower and I on the horse-rake, shaking up the windrows.

Then help came. Two young Englishmen in early summer had taken up homesteads, built their shacks, and then had gone off to work on a near-by ranch. Now the round-up was over and they were back at home; Alfred Greaves about a mile south and west of us, and Gordon Henson a little farther on.

Seeing our new house they naturally came over to investigate. Apparently they didn't find us repulsive so they hung around, for company, helped cock and stack the hay and gave Homer a hand with the new barn. A good-sized barn it was, big enough for our horses and cows, but it had no proper roof; only flat boards with a heavy overthatch of hay. But it served. The roof was another of the many things to be done next summer when we would have time.

After using odds and ends to build a chicken-house we were ready to tighten up the house for winter. We got the clapboarding done and built a proper chimney with bricks and lime brought out from Carstairs. Inside sheeting was postponed; it seemed a shame to spoil our soft, grey walls. Alfred and Gordon volunteered to go to the mines for coal. Nobody owned that coal. You just dug it out of a creek-bank some fifty miles away and came home rejoicing. Good coal too! With it blazing in the big range and in the little Quebec heater upstairs the north winds were defied and a proper comfort was our lot.

They were fine boys, of good family. Alfred's father was a clergyman. So were his two brothers. He himself had been well started on his Divinity course when he decided to go farming in Western Canada. Gordon also had deserted a normal business career at home for "a spot of adventure." Neither was a "remittance man," sent away for the peace and honour of the family and with little taste for hard labour. These boys were willing, diligent and superbly green. They knew all about proper dessert and salad forks, but hay-forks were

17

strange, outlandish tools. Harness was a mystery. So was carpentry. They drove nails on the trial-and-error method. But they were eager to learn, and learned everything well.

I'm sure that their cooking was rudimentary, for they looked at my bread and biscuits, my custards, my fried breast of wild duck, my angel cake and pies with uplifted eyebrows and a great longing—frequently satisfied, for we enjoyed their company. Homer helped them with their sod-breaking, lent them horses and gear, so the obligations balanced and there was no talk of cash settlement.

As the days shortened and the early frosts sparkled in the moonlight the after-supper hours at our place often had a musical flavour. We all sang fairly well and Alfred had an autoharp, plunking out the major and minor chords and making an excellent accompaniment. For sentiment, "Silver Threads Among the Gold," "Old Black Joe," "When You and I Were Young, Maggie," or "Home, Sweet Home." But this last was too tough. I kept thinking of my invalid father and my sisters; Homer, of his mother and "the folks"; the boys, of Piccadilly Circus, or The High in Oxford, or of quiet church yards under the yews. So we put that song on the reserve list and never brought it out again. To this day when the radio brings in its first strains I turn the button—and quickly.

But there were other songs; music hall favourites of the old days, such as "What Am I Going To Do Now?" or "The Man That Broke The Bank At Monte Carlo." These and other frivolities were in Gordon's repertoire and he sang with exultation—if only to see the slight vexation in Alfred's face and feel it in the accompaniment. On Sunday nights there were hymns as well, excerpts from "Hymns, Ancient and Modern" or from the older Moody and Sankeys. So we had pleasant evenings as well as busy days, and I can remember occasions when the oatmeal porridge in a double-boiler, ready to re-heat for breakfast disappeared long before bedtime.

Late in the fall Free came up again bringing the binder

and other machinery which he had used in taking off our North Dakota crop. With him came the three nephews, for the youngest had followed his brothers, ready to "homestead" not too far from us, and from a neighbour whose daughter had attractions for the eldest. So we weren't lonesome, and indeed never had been.

Besides there were the Caves. Billy Cave and his lively little wife had come to the district in the previous spring, bringing with them from England all that any family could need. They had lived in a shack until they could get a house built, but calamity came. A prairie fire roared down upon them and they were lucky to escape while the shack and everything in it were burned. A near-by rancher took them in; Mrs. Cave as a cook and Billy as a rider, and now, with a little money ahead they came back to their homestead and made a fresh start. Mrs. Cave was the first woman I saw in the three months we had been on the prairie, and we were excellent friends.

Going to Carstairs was all right for the men, but I had no time for a long eighteen miles each way, at perhaps five miles an hour. There was little or nothing to see if I had gone. I will admit, however, that to be eighteen miles from a post office or a telegraph line is too far. Also to be that distance from a doctor is much too far. Homer was as well as he had ever been but I could not forget his bout with pneumonia. I had heard that some people were subject to that disease, that there was some undiscoverable weakness of the lungs that invited it. So I was always standing sentry over him lest he might catch cold.

I knitted for him assiduously. I made him a chamois vest. I compelled him to change clothes or socks whenever he got wet. And while he pooh-poohed and tut-tutted, smiling, he met my requirements and came through the winter without either a sniffle or a cough. And still I worried, being young and foolish; not yet knowing that worry never eased any burden or averted any disaster.

19

IV

In four months we had done much towards making a home, and it was time for a breathing-spell. Christmas was only three weeks away and some shopping was desirable. If only we could have a day or two in Calgary—but that was a dream. Cows were to be fed and milked, cream had to be churned, eggs had to be gathered. Then came Alfred one night with a young English friend from one of the ranches. The friend was willing to take over the chores if we cared to go. We cared.

The weather had been gracious all through the autumn. Morning frosts had been dissolved by sunshine and no fierce winds had uncoiled themselves in the hills for a good blow at the invaders of the prairie. So we decided to drive to Calgary, sixty miles southwestward over the horizon; and no roads to restrict our wandering. The democrat was sound, though showing signs of wear and tear, and the driving team, Pet and Flora, in good fettle. With Alfred and Gordon in the back seat, Homer and I up front and a full lunch basket convenient the journey would be a sort of gipsy progress.

The night before the start it turned cold and there was a "skiver" of snow. Feeling sure that the mild spell was over I put on an extra petticoat and wore my dogskin coat and Persian lamb cap (parting gifts from relatives in London). I had an extra pair of stockings and my heavy overshoes. They had no zippers and there was no fur around the tops, so they were not really smart. My fur gauntlets were much smarter. Full-armed against the weather I climbed over the wheel to a seat beside my husband. We took a south-south-west bearing and got under way at seven o'clock in the morning. A gopher, shivering on his little mound on the sunny side of the barn squeaked a timid farewell.

Tom McGee had a ranch down the Rosebud valley some seven miles away; that was to be our first objective. The prairie was a little too bumpy for speedy travel and the horses had to keep a wary eye for badger holes, but we made progress. The McGees' house was strategically placed where Stony Creek joined the Rosebud, so that visitors, from whatever direction they approached, had to ford one of the streams. We crossed with no trouble and got acquainted with Mrs. McGee, a dark, quick-eyed and smiling little Scottish woman, eager to offer hospitality. But we weren't hungry yet. All we wanted was a chart of direction. Which way should we go in order to reach Calgary in reasonable time?

Mr. McGee cogitated in his Glasgow way and directed us to the Carleton ranch, a fairly large "outfit" almost due south. From there onward steering orders would certainly be available. I noticed that the McGees saw nothing extraordinary in our idea of driving to Calgary. Indeed they seemed to respect us and cultivated our acquaintance. Tom had had a meal at our place some weeks before while out riding for stray

21

cattle. Now both he and Mrs. McGee affirmed that they would call on us soon after our return. "And you'll come back this way, of course," was Mrs. McGee's last word. And so, across Stony Creek and up the high bank of the coulée.

It was a clear day and the mountains never looked finer. Above them a mass of cloud had a beautiful yellow tinge which we greatly admired. The prairie was less bumpy and about noon we came on a spacious house surrounded by corrals where Mr. Carleton, a bachelor, lived. He had four or five men working around the place and a blithe young housekeeper "did for" them all. We stayed for dinner—our lunch basket still untouched—and were directed south and west by a route which ultimately would bring us to the Reid ranch, some twenty miles from Calgary. Even yet there was no proper road, only a trail, that sometimes after a half-mile or so died out in the grasses. There were plenty of cow-paths and side trails which we were warned to avoid since they led nowhere in particular, and we were bound for Calgary.

But from the Reid ranch onward a trail was well-defined and we were able to move more briskly. About five o'clock in the afternoon we descended the long hill on the eastern out- skirts of Calgary and came trotting to First Street East where Chief English lived. I had a hearty welcome from Mrs. English and Bess—now boarding at home—while Homer was finding hotel stabling for the horses, and a room for the boys. They were invited by the Chief to spend the evening with us at his house.

I shan't forget that evening, so rich in kindness and hospitality. The Chief was almost excited when he learned that Alfred was a musician. He himself was fond of music, though not a performer, and had one of the old-fashioned player-attachments in front of his fine piano. "Here," he said in his most vigorous tone—and it could be vigorous—"get this damn' contraption out of the road and let Alfred play." And

22

play he did; all the old songs with ardour and expression, until nearly midnight.

"It will be mild tomorrow," the Chief said as the boys were leaving. "I suppose you noticed the Chinook arch." That, we discovered, was the yellow cloud overhanging the mountain peaks which had interested us in the afternoon. Even as he was speaking a soft, velvet wind was flowing over the city. Next morning all the snow was gone and the gutters flowing with water. As I passed the Alberta Hotel, Windsor chairs on the sidewalk were occupied by a dozen men in shirtsleeves, while I sweltered in my dogskin coat.

I had left off the extra petticoat, the stockings and the over-shoes, even the smart fur gauntlets, and had gladly replaced the fur cap with my best hat, which for some unconscious, prophetic reason I had brought in a paper bag. Still I was too hot and stayed too hot as I carried my lengthy shopping-list about the town. The Hudson's Bay store, then at Centre Street and Eighth Avenue, literally welcomed me with open doors. All other shops I patronized did likewise. But the Chinook was a sweet and lovely wind which made me think of the winds of North Dakota; it was so different.

On the next morning we hitched up for the journey home and the democrat had much more in it than the builders ever could have dreamed it could contain. Chief English had got us a dozen currant bushes. "Sure, plant 'em," he had said. "The ground isn't frozen yet and they'll be all right." Also he had remembered Alfred saying that he would like to get a few pigeons. Here they were, a dozen or more, in a basket-hamper with a lid, burbling a cooing protest. Where the Chief had found them we didn't know and he didn't tell. If he had not been a stern officer of the law we might have thought darkly of someone robbing a loft. But no, he must have bought them and paid for them, like a Christian.

"Where'll we put them?" I exclaimed.

23

"Hang the basket on behind," he replied. "Here, wait a minute." He popped into the house and popped out again with a length of clothes-line and the basket was secured.

We had a case of canned tomatoes, a case of canned salmon, various other groceries, including the makings of a Christmas cake and pudding, for the Caves were coming to dinner on Christmas Day. These many things, together with our eight feet jammed the democrat tight. Just before we left the Chief said to Homer, "You'll need a couple of coyote hounds. I'll ship 'em up by way of Carstairs."

With his hearty voice in our ears we trotted eastward along Ninth Avenue, climbed the long hill and hit the north trail. Soon after we passed Reid's ranch and were again on the bumpy prairie we heard a crack, and the hind wheels started to lean inwards. The boys got out and investigated. The democrat had balked. Like the last straw that broke the camel's back our hamper of pigeons (probably) had bent the rear axle. It wasn't broken, but it might break at any time unless we humoured it. So from there on to the Carleton ranch, where some makeshift repair might be expected, two of the boys walked, taking regular turns every couple of miles. It was a slow and uneasy pilgrimage, not improved when we got to Carleton's. Mr. Carleton was away and the men about the place could suggest nothing to ease our difficulty.

"If we had a rail or a pole—" mused Homer.

But poles were scarce just then and no one would take the responsibility of picking one off a corral for our advantage. So we pushed on towards McGee's, not cheerfully; the boys still walking to ease the axle. It was dark when we splashed through the creek and halted.

"You'll stay all night," said Tom, "and we'll fix you up in the morning." That evening we discovered that both Mr. and Mrs. McGee were singers; not the ordinary sort like us, but real ones with concert experience in Scotland. Tom was a gold-medallist. We heard "Ye Banks and Braes" and "Caller

24

Herrin'" and "Mary Morrison" and plenty more, so that joy was in our hearts as we looked forward to a musical winter time.

Next morning one end of a long pole was lashed to the front of our chariot and passed back over the front axle to support the injured member. Now all hands could get aboard and after negotiating the creek ford we managed our last six miles. Home again from a furrin shore!

That poor old democrat had a history. Since for two years it was the only light vehicle in the neighbourhood everybody borrowed it from time to time as need arose, and frequently something went wrong. Once when the Carstairs blacksmith was called on again to deal with its defects he looked sternly at Homer and said, "Who owns this democrat anyway? I've repaired it for nearly everybody in your district, but you bring it in most often."

"Is it yours?" Homer nodded. "Well, it certainly has been through the wars."

V

We planted our currant bushes, not hopefully, for December was more than half gone. By New Year's Day the weather sharpened and before long I could have worn in the house my dogskin coat, my extra petticoat, and even my overshoes all day long. But again the Chinook arch appeared and the velvet wind blew. As near-by bachelors dropped in for the evening to toast their shins before our range and to fill the house with pungent, blue pipe-smoke I heard all the tall tales of the foot-hills about the Chinook; such as the one about the man gallop-ping his horses so as to keep the front bob of his sleigh on the snow while the hind bob was in water and the dog running behind was drowned. ·

These bachelor-sessions were jolly occasions, usually coming to a ten o'clock climax with coffee and doughnuts. For the Gregory boys and Godfrey Jones, and Joe Oswald, the Rogerses and the Wigles had a rich fund of ranch stories, and Gordon Henson remembered the milder tales of the music-hall comics, and someone had heard of the latest exploit of Bob Edwards of the *Eyeopener* and my husband recalled odd characters of the Ontario scene, and Alfred had his autoharp.

The smoke never bothered me, for my four brothers at home were walking chimneys, and while for years I never smoked there came a time when cigarettes began to be offered as a social courtesy to women as well as to men. I suppose, in my most abandoned time, one package did me for a month or more.

As I look back I am astonished at the contrast with present days in the matter of liquor. I have no doubt that every one of these bachelors who favoured us with their company would take a drink now and then with the usual satisfaction. But they could leave it alone. They never had one at our place for we had silent opinions on that subject. None of them ever brought a flask. I never saw one of them drunk, or even a little "lighted." Even at the parties of later years—and they became rather frequent as new people came in—everybody seemed to be happy without alcoholic aid.

Moreover there was marked disapproval of intemperate drinking. The comment "He's a boozer" was a final criticism. Sometimes we played cards, though not often, and always the game was Five Hundred, not Poker. In our time most of the bachelors were English or Scottish lads coming from good homes. Some were well-to-do, working because they liked it rather than because they had to. There was no trace of the "wild west" atmosphere. Not once did I see a cowboy or a ranch hand with a revolver, or even a belt-holster.

They were sportsmen, of course, riding with hounds after coyotes, or pinking jack-rabbits with a .22 rifle, or downing wild ducks or prairie chicken with breach-loading shotguns, or going to the foothills with a Winchester for moose or red deer. But they didn't shoot at one another. There was a perpetual closed season for men. No doubt the omnipresence and omnipotence of the Mounted Police damped the exuberance of a few reckless figures familiar with the looser customs of Montana and Wyoming.

Some of our bachelor friends had mothers overseas, and a number of them used to write to me from time to time expressing a wholly unnecessary gratitude. More than that, I remember presents of tins of cocoa, or caddies of tea, or bolts of a superfine flannel which left me embarrassed as well as grateful. My husband and I were doing nothing for these boys but enjoying their company, and this is no affectation of modesty. To us they were fun.

New Year's dinner at the Caves' was thrilling. There was great scarcity of tableware and a lack of space, for their new shack had only one room, the bed at one end being concealed by curtains. But there was no scarcity of food or of laughter. Mrs. Cave was a housekeeper "of pairts." Everything was polished and shining and no speck of dust could be found. Ralph Woods, a near-by bachelor, dropped in and was rebuked. He had a habit of hooking his heels on the rung of his chair when he began to talk. The hostess tolerated the error for a while, and then spoke out. "Ralph Woods, put your feet on the floor. You're scraping all the paint off my chairs." She was a direct little body but good-humoured, and cheerfully endured our teasing.

So the winter dragged away. Homer fenced-in a garden plot, plowed and harrowed it, while I planted potatoes and all the ordinary vegetable seeds. Flower beds were planned and the currant bushes, rebuking our doubts, soon displayed a vigorous life.

One man, even with a gang-plow and wide harrows, couldn't expect to break enough land in one brief spring to get a living-yield of grain. So we got some two hundred heifers on shares, for herding and "wintering." Half the calves to come were to be ours as the beginning of a modest herd. That necessitated the building of a six-foot corral on the southern side of the barn and the planting of a snubbing post for the branding. I saw one calf branded. If I had seen the operation a second time I probably would have gone behind a stack to be sick. Even a necessary cruelty, seemed to me unnecessarily cruel.

We bought the east quarter-section adjoining ours, intending to cultivate it first, reserving most of the west quarter for pasture. There was plenty of unoccupied land north and south as well. But the cattle had to be herded continually, otherwise, at any time they might take a notion to go back to their former stamping-ground. Once they had been winter-fed at our corral they would stay at home. But until then, if one began musing on old times, stopped grazing and set out for Olds, the whole herd would follow at a fast walk until a rider headed them off and drove them back.

We had a succession of herders, mostly English, and occasionally "dumb." I remember one particularly. My husband gave him the most careful instruction, explaining that if the cattle once started they would go northwest. The boy had ridden out one morning to watch the herd grazing about Hill's Lake, a considerable slough to the north of us, behind a rise of land. He had a book with him, so I assume that he dismounted, started reading, and fell asleep. He had a positive talent for sleeping. When he awoke the cattle had disappeared. In great alarm he rode for miles—to the *East* and returned to say that he hadn't been able to find them. Homer had to drop what he was doing and spend two full days in the saddle before he could get them back home.

In the intervals between "dumb" herders I substituted, doing my housework with my saddled horse at the back door, ready for instant departure. I loved riding, and only once was I thrown. I was coming up from our creek to the barn at an easy canter and had slipped my feet out of the stirrups in preparation for dismounting. Something in the grass frightened my horse. He shied and I shot off his back to a sitting posture on the ground while my husband leaned against the barn and laughed and laughed until I wanted to shake him.

That spring we had a considerable accession of new settlers, mostly Americans from Washington State, and our social interests widened. Some of these people were charming and enduring friends. Others were, perhaps, less attractive, and a few were grotesques. Ten miles north of us a group from Illinois appeared and put down roots in the country. Their descendants are still there, continuing to be the salt of their neighbourhood.

In other directions some were less savoury. I think of a girl, over-fat, over-dressed, over-garrulous and over-flighty who called herself "Jumbo" and made eyes at any riders who happened along. Most of them laughed and rode on.

I think of the "superior" woman who was always inviting us to come for a meal. When we took her at her word she served little or nothing. Once we were formally invited for dinner at six-thirty. There was a plate of small and fancy sandwiches for four of us and a cup of tea each. Homer became smilingly ironical, thanking her for her generous hospitality and insisting that he had had plenty, thank you, and couldn't eat another bite. He had a habit of doing that sort of thing with a straight face and keeping the rest of us in suppressed stitches.

I think of the shifty, tight-lipped old man who accused my husband of stealing a calf and sent for the Mounted Police. One of our bull-calves of a wandering temperament had been tied up in our corral. One day he broke the rope and departed, having found friends in the other herd. When one of our men went after "Ropy" and brought him home the old man swore that the calf was his and that Homer was a so-and-so, if not a what-do-you-call-it. Unfortunately for the accuser the beast bore our brand, as well as part of our rope. The con-

30

stable, knowing the man of old, just laughed, winked solemnly at Homer and rode away.

We knew personally Pawpukeesis the great boaster that Longfellow celebrated. Or if not the actual character, one like him. This earnest soul, late of Washington, could reel off absurd lies by the hour, confidently expecting everyone to believe him. His report of "the big stone from Mars" that had dropped on his farm "back home and dug a hole fifteen feet across, by God," was a mere sample. The big game he had shot, the marvels he had seen, the great men he had known were multitudinous, and again the boys just laughed and rode away. All but Homer and our nephew Earl. These slyboots always expressed complete belief and solemnly stirred the man to more and livelier inventions. They found him most entertaining.

Most of the settlers from the United States were people of commonsense who realized that they were now in a different country with, perhaps, different ideas and were eager to conform. Some were of another kidney, imagining that they were the people and that wisdom would die with them.

After the new Province of Alberta was set up, in 1905, school sections were formed and trustees elected to build the schools and choose teachers. In the days of organization a meeting of neighbours was called to discuss school affairs and one of the older women from south of the border was active in criticism. Pending the establishment of Normal Schools, teachers holding certificates from other provinces of Canada had been welcomed, perhaps more confidently than a few from the States.

"I'll tell you what's wrong with this country," said the critic. "There are too many foreigners from Ontario."

VI

DURING our first summer on the prairie, even before the house was built a vigorous young man rode up one day from the south, dismounted and introduced himself. He was a Divinity student, improving his college vacation by field work, based on the hamlet of Crossfield, the next station south of Carstairs. He has been holding occasional services at Cochrane's house, about six miles southwest of us, and invited us to attend the following Sunday afternoon.

We accepted warmly, for at home we both had been church-minded, and here we had found our Sundays rather bare and lean. So in a cheerful mood we rode across country and at last joined a dozen-or-so other folk assembled. We waited, and waited, decorously enough, but no preacher appeared, so there was nothing to do but get introduced all around and ride home.

Later we learned that the young man had got lost; couldn't find Cochrane's or any other house, until, by accident he came upon a ranch in the Rosebud valley and could chart a course for Crossfield. The rolling prairie always was a problem for travellers. Houses or shacks were small and might be wholly concealed by rising ground until one was only a few hundred yards away. The lack of trees—and even bush-clumps grew only in the coulées—gave no landmarks for a rider. All he could do was to take a general direction from the sun, keep on going and trust his luck. The young man's luck, evidently, had been bad, and he didn't test it again, at least in our direction. October came and he went back East to college.

We had a light snowfall that autumn and one day a young man came whooping along on skis; the first I had ever seen. He seemed to be an expert in what, to me, always seems to be an awkward sport. Naturally we invited him to dinner; every stranger was a dinner-guest. He also invited us to a service in a settler's house, but we got word that the arrangement was cancelled. He also had been called back to college.

Early the next summer came another budding minister, just appointed to Crossfield and the prairie-at-large. His name was Johnson and he was organizing a circuit of preaching-places. Would we be willing to have services in our house every other Sunday? We surely would, though doubting if our place were large enough. He assured us that it was the largest in a radius of six miles or so, and certainly the most central. So the arrangement was completed.

He would come out on Saturday evening, stay all night, preach at eleven, have dinner, preach in a school eight miles away at two, at a house farther on at four, and get back to Crossfield for an evening service at seven. Obviously he wasn't lazy. But he was inclined to be dilatory. On the first Saturday evening we waited for him until after ten o'clock and then went to bed. About half-past eleven he arrived. Our nephews were with us that night and all the beds were full. But my husband and I lugged the red couch upstairs and set it in the little hall-way where a variety of things were kept. Just above his head hung a side-saddle which some Ontario friends had given me, with the mistaken notion that I could use it. They didn't know that it was a thing no self-respecting western horse would wear. We got the bedding arranged and as a parting advice Homer said, "If you get a nightmare you're welcome to use the saddle." The nephews in near-by beds laughed aloud and from that moment the preacher's dignity was abated.

He proved to be good company, though with a consuming interest in horses. He could "talk horse" longer and more enthusiastically than a jockey. Of course Homer and nephew Earl stimulated him to talk more horse, and still more, until I would come to his rescue by changing the subject. Privately I rebuked them, but it didn't "take." They insisted that the young man didn't know he was being "kidded" so what was the difference? Especially as they were getting so fine a variety of veterinary information—mostly wrong.

I won't say that Mr. Johnson was a great pulpit orator, but he was sincere and friendly of spirit and we liked him. The congregation often numbered a score besides ourselves, and was made up chiefly of people who had been church folk at their former homes. Some came six or seven miles and couldn't be expected to ride back without some refreshment. So, almost invariably, the moment "Amen" was said I skipped out to put on the kettle. The young preacher had to make an early start for his next appointment, so I set the table with speed and generally all the congregation stayed for dinner. More than once I had three sittings at my dining-table; a happy arrangement since we got acquainted more quickly.

Mr. and Mrs. Bryson were always present. He was an Englishman past middle age, a little more stately than neces-sary and less considerate of his wife, or of any woman, than the men of Canada usually are. Alfred and Gordon had small patience with his airs, but his wife evidently was impressed by them and seemed to enjoy her subordinate position. She always called him "Mr. Bryson" in a respectful tone and mentioned his likes and dislikes as if they were important.

"At home Mr. Bryson was very fond of plovers' eggs. Of course there are none here, but you'd be surprised how like them are the prairie-chickens' eggs. Frequently in the early morning I come on a nest, and he enjoys them so much."

Her dresses, all home-made of strange fabrics and patterns were of Eighteenth Century style. The fullness of the skirts was a marvel and she always had a pocket as long as her arm. She could carry anything in it; her knitting, an extra pair of woollen hose, a length of white linen "to make dickeys for Mr. Bryson," a tanned gopher-skin or two to make ear-muffs for Mr. Bryson's cap, or even a few crusty buns which often I pressed upon her, since she—and Mr. Bryson—were so fond of them.

One Sunday morning she was late for the service, and came in while Mr. Johnson had just got nicely into his sermon. As she came in the door, not realizing the situation, she said in her precise, high-pitched tones, "I'm afraid I'm a little late, but we were detained. Mr. Bryson had to go down to the pasture; one of our cows was having a calf." The solemnity of the service seemed to suffer a sharp decline. Soon afterwards the Brysons sold their homestead and faded out of view.

Mr. Johnson regretted that some of the settlers didn't seem interested enough to come to the services and he hadn't had a chance to meet them. He wondered if some social event could be arranged; one that might bring everybody. We thought it was an idea and Homer said, "What about a box-social?"

He agreed that nobody could consider anything specially religious about a box-social, and if he could catch men by guile, there was Scriptural authority for it.

"What about the money from the sale of the boxes?" we asked. "Could he find some good use for it?"

He could. His congregation at Crossfield was building a church and any additional funds would be welcome.

So we fixed a date and passed the word around by herders, cowboys, or neighbours going to Carstairs. The programme was no problem. Prairie custom settled that. Everyone present would be expected to do something; sing, or recite, make a speech, or tell a story. But singers would need an accompaniment and we feared that Alfred's autoharp might be inadequate. The Sieberts, seven miles away, had a small reed organ. Maybe they would lend it. One of the boys hitched a horse to a stoneboat and went over to see. "Certainly," said the Sieberts, and the little organ went visiting.

Since our house was anything but spacious we moved the heavier furniture into the barn, brought in planks and made a seat all around the walls. People who might come from the east could not see our house until they topped a small rise, so we tied a lighted lantern on a long pole and set it up. Over fifty people turned up, twelve of them being girls or women, about four men to each one. So we fixed up boxes for half the men. The programme was good. Harry Schofield had a well-trained baritone voice; others sang, and one of the girls played good accompaniments. As a climax Homer stood on the stairs and sold the boxes by auction.

The earnestness shown by a group of bachelors in bidding up Mary Long's box so that her "steady fellow" couldn't afford to buy it may have had an irreligious quality. Also some chagrin was observable on the face of a lad who had bid lavishly only to find that his lunch-partner was not the girl he expected but a leathery old cowboy with a sorrel moustache and a bobbing Adam's apple. But Mr. Johnson got acquainted with everybody and took away with him something over forty-eight dollars to sweeten his building fund.

Since an evening party had been manageable an afternoon gathering should be easy. Again at Mr. Johnson's suggestion we decided to have a picnic. Without a telephone or telegraph wire, a post office or a community store, without even a blacksmith nearer than eighteen miles one would think that spreading the news would be difficult. But a mysterious grape-vine system seemed to be in operation.

My uncle, Sam Wheaton from Ontario, had come to visit us and was in a perpetual dither about the way things were done. The vast emptiness in all directions seemed to put him in a daze. He couldn't understand allowing cattle to graze on land we didn't own. He wasn't used to corrals and snubbing posts, and Western saddles, and horses that came when the owners whistled, and gophers, and red-tailed hawks with no high trees to nest in.

"A picnic!" he exclaimed when we told him what was in prospect. "A picnic, without people?"

"Oh, we'll have a few," we replied. He took another look around the horizon and shook his dear old head in doubt.

Next morning I was in a carnival of cooking, turning out cakes, cookies and pies, shredding cold chicken for sandwiches and squeezing lemons for future lemonade.

"What's the idea?" he said in puzzled tone as he saw the result of my labours spread out on the big table.

"Getting ready for the picnic. We don't want anybody to go short."

"Picnic!" he replied. "I thought you were fooling."

"Certainly not. You'll see."

"Where'll the people come from?"

"Oh, 'round and about."

They began to come about two o'clock; people in lumber wagons, people on horseback, suddenly appearing from all directions, riding up from the creek-bed, dismounting, throwing the bridle reins over the horses' heads and coming together in knots for talk and laughter.

37

"The horses aren't tied," said Uncle Sam. "Won't they go away?"

"Where would they go?" returned Homer. "The grass around here is all right, and it's shady by the stacks. These are cayuses and know when they're well off—nothing to do for a while but stick around."

Uncle Sam looked down past the spring and said suddenly, "What's that?"

It was a wagonload of young fellows all dressed alike; the baseball team from Kneehill Creek, nearly thirty miles away, to the northeast, coming to have a game with the Carstairs nine, which might be expected at any time from eighteen miles west. Uncle Sam pushed back his hat and scratched his head. Clearly the circumstances were beyond credibility.

Well over a hundred people attended that picnic and we had an abundance of entertainment. One of the cowboys had brought a couple of bucking horses and several had a try at riding them. An obstacle horse-race was a lively spectacle. Foot races were arranged for the younger fry. A quartet off to one side pitched horseshoes with strained attention and careful measurement after each "end." On a platform which my husband had rigged up a young Englishman named Hepburn sang comic songs and did a nonsense monologue, Mr. Johnson and several others made speeches, without saying anything of importance—an ideal accomplishment before a mixed crowd—and the ball game was exciting, although I have no remembrance which team won. But the greatest interest of all was in getting acquainted with one another. Then came supper on the grass with a boilerful of hot coffee to wash it down. Soon afterwards one party and another withdrew for the long ride homeward, and by sunset we were alone, to enjoy the continuing astonishment of Uncle Sam.

Mr. Hepburn and Alfred's brother Christopher (also present) were young clergymen who had volunteered in England for missionary service in Western Canada. After their

38

UNIVERSITY OF WINNIPEG
PORTAGE & BALMORAL
WINNIPEG 2. MAN.   CANADA

visit with Alfred, Christopher was appointed to the parish of Pine Lake, and later a crowd of us drove up there, some fifty miles, on a two weeks' camping expedition, to renew acquaintance. After a year or two Christopher returned to England. Mr. Hepburn served some of the lumber-camps west of Edmonton and we didn't see him again.

There was a stern, almost terrible conventionality about Uncle Sam. Perhaps he might have served as a symbol of the Ontario spirit of his time. He was disturbed at the thought of a clergyman singing comic songs and smoking a pipe. But he was positively flustered when Mr. Hepburn went about bareheaded. Everybody else wore a hat. Why should this young man defy all custom and refuse? The morning and evening airs out here were chilly; why didn't he catch cold? Any intelligent person would, and yet Mr. Hepburn was singularly intelligent. Here was another of the grave problems that made life so complicated.

It was bad enough when the man went bareheaded at a picnic. But the day came when Uncle Sam was leaving us to go to Edmonton and then homeward. Mr. Hepburn elected to go with him as far as Innisfail. For this journey he was still bareheaded. "Hasn't he *got* a hat?" murmured Uncle Sam. "Did he cross the Atlantic without one? What's the matter with the fellow, anyway?" And so, departed, in an aura of question-marks.

I believe that this picnic was the beginning of an annual institution called Sports Day which is celebrated every summer in all the villages of that region. We had one every year as long as we were in the neighbourhood and its popularity never waned.

Mr. Johnson was back again the next summer and by that time a school some four miles away was available for a Sunday service. Soon after we had the use of the Davis School, much nearer. In time we got a reed organ which gave a lift to the singing. Following Mr. Johnson other students came and went, until Mr. Gratz, a settler of uncommon intelligence and with vigour as a speaker, became a sort of unofficial pastor. He was unconventional in his manner and often when he had driven home a point of importance he would turn to my husband and say, "Isn't that so, Jackson?"

His family inherited his mental vigour. A son and a daughter came to prominence in New York; one as a physician, the other as chief dietitian for a chain of restaurants. Another daughter, a gold medallist in mathematics and physics, became one of the ablest and most favourably known high school teachers in the province.

Now that the road allowances were being fenced off and new settlers were arriving the time for large herds of cattle was past. We sold off all but enough for our own available pasture and turned to grain growing.

The democrat was decrepit and we had notified an Ontario brother-in-law, a carriage-builder, that we were about ready for a top-buggy. He shipped it, and, with his wife, Homer's sister, came out to uncrate it and to have a look at what we were doing. Perhaps we had some traces of sinful pride when we hitched up and went driving in a shiny top-buggy with yellow wheels; the only one in a radius of perhaps twenty miles.

VII

In the Rosebud Valley Godfrey Jones built his shack, made it comfortable within its two rooms and started building a nice herd of cattle. He was a young Englishman, blondish, blue-eyed, humorous and lean of talk. From the day he hung his front door it never was locked. If he were absent any rider passing that way was welcome to drop in and cook a meal and smoke a pipe or two. And the fact was widely known.

One evening three cowboys came "by-along" as they would say, went in the shack and found a sign on the cupboard door, "Grub here." They were hungry after a long ride aiming at Olds, so they fired-up the stove, put on the coffee pot and had a satisfying snack.

"I wish the owner would come back," said one of them. "Down the line I heard that his name's Jones. His coffee is dam' good and I'd like to say, 'Thank you',"

The others agreed as they sat about the stove smoking their pipes. One of them thought he could do with a bit of shut-eye on the floor.

While they were talking another cowboy came in asking, "Are you the chaps that owns this dump?"

No; they were just passing through. The fellow had left a sign inviting them to make free—"a kind of a white guy."

"Any objection to my horning in on this?" asked the stranger, as he reached for the coffee-pot and a cup.

"That's up to you. We have to get along. We were just wondering if it would be all right to leave a dollar or so to cover what we ate."

"It might, and it mightn't," the stranger thought. "He isn't keeping a hotel, you know. After all, his door's open and most of the boys up and down this coulée are kind of free. Myself, I think I'll bed down here and explain to him later. If he turns up before morning I'll give him half his own bed."

The trio—admiring the stranger's nerve—moved out and began to tighten their saddle-girths. But they didn't leave. A voice came from the front door, "Bring in your bed-rolls, boys; it's all right. This is my dump. I'm Jones."

This lad was one of our Rosebud bachelors, and a good friend. He had a habit of inviting five or six for Sunday dinner, and frequently we were of the company. Our carriage-building brother-in-law and his wife, known as "Jack'nMary"—one word, since they were one flesh—were invited one Sunday with us and another couple.

They looked on with surprise as Godfrey set the table, flipping white granite plates along the white oilcloth tablecover, and planting at proper intervals the granite cups and silver flatware. Their surprise was greater when he bore in a sirloin roast of beef, mashed potatoes and canned corn which he had prepared himself, and all cooked to perfection. Where he got the apple pies was his secret, but he whipped the cream for them and made the coffee. No woman was to be seen.

42

All through dinner he led with the stories and the laughter, and afterwards supervised the toss-ups which decided which men were to wash the dishes. The lot fell on my husband and Jack, the latter not practised in the art. Mary observed the operation with a kindling eye, and said as we drove home, "I didn't think he could do it; wait till I get him home—and I never ate so much in my life."

Then there was Joe Oswald, who, with the Gregory boys and the Wigles organized the bachelors' parties, as a return for the hospitality of settlers' wives. Twice in the winter the word would go forth. Joe had a big house and abundant room for sixty or seventy guests; settlers and their wives for miles around. Some would play cards. Some would just sit around and talk. Some, on demand, would sing, or tell stories. And then would come the lunch. Graniteware plates and cups would be passed around, and then appeared all the delicacies that could be brought up from Calgary and supplemented by the boys; piles of chicken sandwiches, cakes of all kinds, boxes of candy, crates of oranges and other fruits, and floods of coffee. But, as I have said before, no liquor. I have no doubt that it was available but privately served.

All who had children at home were loaded down with dainties for them and I have been told that always enough was left over to keep the bachelors living high for a month or more. Always, but on one occasion, when a couple of tame bears got loose, went through a cellar-window and ate themselves into a dyspeptic state.

I have heard that in other regions where ranch land was being turned into farm holdings cattlemen were often resentful and contemptuous of all settlers. That was never so in our district; perhaps because the big coulées were free for grazing. There was a community spirit and a wide range of personal friendships.

After the first three-year round-up, when the boys had money, they began to think of the girls they left behind them.

Godfrey Jones brought a dark-eyed beauty from England who played the piano "like Billy-oh" as one of the boys said, and also sang well. Within ten years they had three fine children. Harry Schofield, himself a singer, married an English soprano of grace and talent who was welcome on any Calgary platform. Even our Alfred, of the autoharp, looked afar to an English country-garden.

Meanwhile school-teachers were appearing in the land; pretty girls from Ontario, from the Maritimes, from the mid-Western States, all creating a widespread yearning among young men. Most of them, at some time or other were at our place, usually brought by a cheerful youth named Sedley Meek who had come up from Nova Scotia. He opened a microscopic general store and became postmaster at Sterlingville, a metropolis of two buildings, the store and a blacksmith's shop. For us, to go only four miles instead of eighteen to post a letter or to get one was luxury indeed.

Alfred got a letter one day to the effect that the girl of his choice had crossed the Atlantic, ostensibly to visit her brother in Manitoba. So Alfred went to Manitoba. After a week or so he notified us that he had been married and would be home on such a day. His new house was all but ready but he had not moved in, so, obviously, the bride would cross the threshold of a one-room shack in which everything would be higgledy-piggledy, as always; for Alfred's genius was not towards the housekeeping arts.

He had told us often of the bride-to-be, daughter of a clergyman of good family, living in a rare old rectory with a proper English garden. I thought of the contrast awaiting her and on the night of her arrival I didn't sleep much. Next morning my husband and I went over to help move the stove and the other "heavies" into the new house, and, of course, to say "How do you do," and "Welcome pretty stranger."

She came out of that shack door radiant. Contrasts were nothing to her. Alfred and his friends were everything. I learned later that she had no knowledge of housekeeping—a fitting mate for Alfred—that she had never even washed dishes. If she had made her own bed, it probably was at boarding school, for at home a housekeeper, two or three maids and a "tweenie" looked after everything. There was a man for the garden.

But she could learn. Many times she came over to our place, a good mile across the prairie, to find out one thing or another, or to pick up this or that recipe. Never once did I hear her complain or see her in the dumps. Before long her house was as smart, her table as bountiful, as any in the neighbourhood. She had three children in that prairie home and held her head high in a proper pride.

In our second summer we built a one-room shack with double bunk and a stove for our hired men, and lathed and plastered the inside of our house. For the floors we got a brown-figured linoleum. I had had enough of carpets at home. So now we were "set" for winter.

From Mrs. Greaves and from the bachelors of the Rosebud I found out why the people of England are not the least among the nations. Rich in courtesy, broad in culture, resolute, wise about the uses of money, ready to adapt themselves to all conditions, and willing to work, either with hand or brain or both—is it any wonder that they withstood with a smile the worst that enemies could do?

There were some odd ones, such as the herdsman we had whose only apparent ability was in playing the piccolo. There were some wasters in the towns, but none in our neighbourhood. But when 1914 came, even these straightened up and marched direct to a recruiting office. Like Gordon Henson a good many were killed. As Bob Edwards wrote, "They may have been green but, by God, they weren't yellow!"

VIII

CLOSE to the ground on virgin land was a carpet of short, matted grass commonly known as prairie wool. It was rich in natural oils; horses and cattle thrived on it. Even in winter they would paw away the snow to get it, and if there were no heavy snow-fall they would come off the range in spring healthy and even fat.

In late fall or early spring when this grass was dry a spark would light it. Then if a wind were blowing trouble began for all settlers. Mention has been made of the fire that destroyed Billy Cave's shack and all his possessions. That blaze ran all the way to Kneehill Creek, thirty miles off. A young man had knocked out the ashes from his pipe. "Behold, how great a matter a little fire kindleth."

Whenever a red glow appeared in the sky men came galloping from all directions in the hope of beating out, or controlling the fire. They would plow a fire-break of six or eight furrows well before some settler's place, then set alight the grass a little distance to windward, watching to see that it didn't leap the furrows. Then as the main fire came up it would die out for lack of fuel.

If a spark were carried over it would be thrashed out by flour or grain sacks; sometimes by clothing if no sacks were convenient. I have heard of one excited fire-fighter calling to a woman, "Take off your petticoat; I'll buy you another," and many times women and children had to take refuge in a slough until the main fire had passed.

Usually the flames rose ten or twelve feet high, and, in a wind, the roar was terrifying. The prairie wool made such a hot fire that long, tough grasses and even low bushes like saskatoons or green willows clustered in the coulées soon were completely consumed.

One day my husband had gone some ten miles northwest of our place to conclude a business deal. I happened to look out in that direction and saw the dangerous light in the sky. Before long neighbours began to come, running their horses. Our hired man got out the gang-plow and a team and started swift work on a fire-break. Others began back-firing while I collected buckets and took them down to the spring. Then I started carrying water to the men. As the fire came nearer I saw Homer with a group of the men, all black with smoke, beating at the grass.

I ran across the fire-break to reach him but got swift orders to get back. "Woman," said one man, "are you crazy? Get on this pony and go back to your house." I was glad enough to do so as already the smoke was getting more dense and the heat of the blaze could be felt. The fire was turned aside from our place and swept by without doing any harm. It didn't even approach the cattle pasturing on the east quarter-section.

That was the only prairie fire to come near us; and it was one too many.

Not far from our place lived the Barnes family who seldom went abroad. For them, life was hard and desperately lean. Clothes were a problem for the mother and for the four or five little girls who were as wild and shy as a covey of partridges. Barnes (which wasn't his name) crooked his elbow too frequently, and by the time his thirst was temporarily slaked too little money was left for necessities. Yet he was a decent soul, dazed by frustration, kind when sober and not offensive when drunk.

Mrs. Barnes was expecting again, and near her time, when I suggested that word should be sent to Mrs. Lane, a woman practised in life's beginnings. She thought that this time she wouldn't have Mrs. Lane, but would manage all right. No doubt she hadn't the means to pay the woman's moderate fee but was too proud to say so.

One night Homer and I had gone to Rodney school to the meeting of a literary society, organized by a few bachelors of the neighbourhood. The feature was a debate; not at all serious, either in subject or in argument and we had a good time. Mrs. Lane happened to be present and I took occasion to tell her of Mrs. Barnes and ask if she would come if we went for her. She consented willingly.

We got home about midnight and at one o'clock came Mr. Barnes. His wife was in labour, and would I come? I protested that I wouldn't be any good, that I knew nothing, and urged him to go at once for Mrs. Lane. No; his wife wanted me.

"It's up to you," said my husband, but I knew by his tone that he had no doubts. I could almost hear him thinking, "You're a woman; and you're needed."

In rebellious mood I dressed, and while still sure that I must refuse got into the wagon. My own child had been born with a doctor and a nurse in attendance. I had been a passive figure in their hands. What I knew or didn't know was of no

48

consequence. Now it was of terrible consequence. So I arrived at the house distinctly "in a state."

The house was a shell, with only one-inch boards between the inside and the sharp weather of February. It was lighted by one small lamp, the flame dimmed by a smoky chimney. Before I had my coat off the weary woman on the bed told me where the carbolic acid and the lysol were, and even then was in pain. Mr. Barnes had gone to the barn to put away the horses. Before he came back the baby was born.

I had never even looked into a doctor's book, but I had overheard, years before, an elderly woman explain to another how to tie the cord. I did so, and then, still scared, I rubbed the child with olive oil, wrapped it in a ragged blanket and laid it on the foot of the bed. There was no other place to lay it, not even a manger, though the house might well have been a stable, so lacking it was in normal furniture. There was only one chair in the place.

"Just twenty minutes more," groaned the mother, again bent in pain. That pain died away—and nothing happened. The woman was semi-conscious; in the dim light she looked ghastly. Her husband said, "There ain't anything you can do, but wait."

I waited a full half-hour, almost an hour. I didn't dare send Barnes with a message to Homer; I refused to be left alone. But I called one of the little girls asleep in the loft. There was no stair, only a barn-ladder. "Get on your things quickly," I commanded. "Tell Mr. Jackson to go for Mrs. Lane and get her here in a hurry."

The child left and I sat by the bed until nearly dawn, worrying, shivering and silently praying. Mr. Barnes, sitting on an upturned box by the stove and occasionally putting in coal was no help. He said something about coffee, but I was not responsive.

At last I heard our rig and went to the door. The horse was white with sweat-foam, and stood trembling as Mrs. Lane

49

and Homer got out. He had been driven at high speed for fourteen miles.

"Wait," I said to Homer. "Things are not right. I want to know what Mrs. Lane thinks." In three minutes I knew. She could do nothing, the condition was too dangerous. We'd have to get the doctor.

Homer changed horses and set out for Carstairs. He found the doctor just leaving on his morning round and exacted a promise that he would come as soon as possible. He arrived that afternoon about four o'clock—just in time, he said. Perhaps all doctors say that, I don't know, but this one was right. I'm sure there were signs of fever after sixteen hours. There were in me.

Within a twenty-hour period Homer had driven 8 miles to Rodney and back, 14 miles to bring Mrs. Lane, and 36 miles for the doctor; 58 miles. And I had always been warning him never to get over-tired, lest he catch cold and the pneumonia devil would be upon us again.

I waited until the doctor said the mother would be all right, and then went home to stumble into bed and give my ragged nerves rest by a wild fit of crying.

The child lived and thrived like his sisters, despite family difficulties. I went there every day for two weeks, and the Barnes family, quite foolishly, regarded me as a sort of benefactor, when in reality I was only an ignorant woman standing around helpless in the face of a crisis.

I have, generally speaking, no quarrel with my elders. They were diligent, full of courage and kind. They taught us children much that was of value in later, as well as in earlier years. But surely they made a mistake in leaving us ignorant about the wonder of new life, the miracle completed when a child is born.

They were silent about birth, as if it were a shameful thing, instead of the shining glory of God revealed. Girls with good mothers were fortunate. But my mother had died before

I was sixteen and the ancient wisdom of the race was never passed on to me.

I am glad to be living in an age when the intelligent, pregnant mother confides in her young children, tells of the joyous prospect of a new baby as the gift of God, and gives them at least some rudimentary instruction on the care and respect due to their bodies as well as their souls.

I was equally inexperienced when called to help prepare for burial, first a young baby, and then an elderly old friend. But other women were there and the grimness of the task was eased by their company and their knowledge. Then I think of the little boy shot to death by a careless companion. Homer made the coffin. We covered it, and then lined it with white satin. We were pioneer people and had to be ready for any emergency.

IX

A CANADIAN PACIFIC RAILWAY branch-construction, nosing its way north from Langdon past Irricana came to a pause about ten miles east of our place. The engineers put an old box-car beside the track as a station and named it Acme. To them the region must have seemed the peak of something or other; nobody knows what. For us, perhaps, the coming of the railway marked the peak of the pioneer period.

Sterlingville immediately lost half its buildings, since the post office, complete with postmaster, removed to Acme. The fact that a mail box was now ten miles away instead of four was not too troublesome to us. Roads were improving, stores were springing up, an elevator was a-building, a doctor had opened an office, and with the railway had come a telegraph line.

More wonderful still, a telephone exchange was established and rural lines radiated from it. Isolation was ended. Instead of talking to the neighbours perhaps twice a month we could speak to them, or they to us, at any moment of the day or night. And the instrument was *used!* Some good women, hungry for speech, listened-in, whether called or not. The news, or rumour of news, over a twenty-mile neighbourhood was everybody's possession. A settler who had a new gramophone record would put it on and call distant friends to listen. Political or other meetings could be arranged in five minutes. Long preparation for social gatherings was no longer necessary.

That gave two of the women an idea; an afternoon party for wives and daughters; not to discuss anything in particular, but rather to get acquainted. One of the two opened her house, and, purposely, the refreshments were kept simple. Two or three monthly meetings were held, until the war came, and a Red Cross Centre in Acme took a dominant place. After the war the original idea was revived and the Grace Guild came into being; an organization without race or creed distinctions, and with no special axes to grind.

But subjects of community interest came up for discussion and sometimes for united action. The Acme cemetery, a wind-bitten square of bald prairie was made less grim by shrubbery and flower beds. Any family in trouble, financial or otherwise, was quietly aided, but best of all the prairie women, rich and poor, old and young, were bound in a fine sisterhood, made closer still when the automobile came to close up distance like a concertina.

From an account of a meeting of the Guild which appeared in the Toronto *Globe and Mail* in 1937, the following paragraphs are quoted:

"In truth this Guild was a Women's Institute, long before the Women's Institutes of eastern Canada had come into being. It was non-sectarian, non-political, non-racial; an organization for friendliness alone. I attended a meeting, held in the four-room house of the latest bride of the neighbourhood. Thirty-seven women were present; some had come fifteen miles. Nine motor cars brought the members and nearly every car had a chair or two strapped on the running-board, for probably Dorothy, in her new nest, wouldn't have enough chairs to serve the company. Such is the thoughtful spirit of the Guild.

"Not being a woman, I sat outside with a couple of men and talked about tumbling mustard and French stinkweed in their relation to agriculture. But I heard the strains of 'He Leadeth Me' which opened the meeting, and of another familiar hymn which closed it. Yet it was not a religious meeting, merely a Grace-ful one. The conference was crowned by refreshments provided by a galaxy of inspired cooks who have all the cream and eggs they want. The men were called in, as critics, and appreciated the privilege. . . . While the trappings of civilization have been steadily put on, the inner soul of civilization, which is simple friendliness and trust, has been nourished by the Grace Guild."

In this region dairying, stock-feeding and grain growing seemed to develop equally. If an early frost softened the wheat to Grade 5 or worse, it was still good for hogs. If a slashing hailstorm cut the grain to rags a few weeks of sunshine gave a crop of green-feed for cattle. Despite wind and weather hens laid eggs, steers fattened, cows gave milk, cream cans went to the butter-factory, and Alberta butter took first prize, year after year at the Toronto Exhibition. So a moderate prosperity came to the diligent; as it usually does.

Tree-planting, begun in the earliest days, continued, enthusiastically sponsored by the Provincial Department of Agriculture and the College farm at Olds. Thus, before many years had passed, nearly every farm had a wind-break of leafy poplars, or karagana hedge, protecting the house and garden. I remember one of the earliest and shyest lads from England, planting and planting with unwearied enthusiasm.

"But when these grow up," I said, "people passing won't be able to see your house."

He nodded. "Then I won't have to wave at them." To this day the house is in umbrageous dimness, but the lad himself is also buried, far away.

Behind one of the farm houses, a shining bungalow on the edge of a small coulée, lies a rock garden of superior design and beauty. The owner dammed the little creek and made an ornamental pond with a toy waterfall leading back to the watercourse. In the middle of the pond is a rock island about the size of a taxicab; on it many strange grasses flourish. White water-lilies are in the pond, and leading up the side of the coulée are three terraces, all-coloured with perennial flowers. The Parks Superintendent of Calgary often drove out, sixty miles, to show this rock-garden to visiting friends. And all this used to be naked prairie over which I have galloped time and again on coyote hunts.

The countryside nowadays between Acme and Carstairs has a thoroughly civilized aspect. The houses are attractive, the barns adequate, the gardens opulent; in late summer the grain is a wavy, golden sea. Cattle still graze in the coulées; not the common range cattle now, but pure-bred Holsteins or Ayrshires. Not many horses are seen. Tractors do the work, often with a girl driving. And in most barns milking machines and separators are driven by put-putting gas engines; to the ease of men and women alike.

Mechanization was a godsend when the second great war called to the young men. As before, they volunteered in a steady procession, and often only one past-age man was left to manage a half-section or more. I know a farm of 920 acres where the farmer's wife, a gracious lady of university training, drove the tractor in harvest time for thirty-nine days. Once she was a school teacher and churned a young farmer's heart until he summoned all his courage and proposed to her. "And so they were married and lived happy ever after."

Has the spirit of the people shown any decline since pioneer days? Are they less friendly, less diligent, less resourceful? I think not. The level of education is higher, for the small regional schools are being consolidated, for better efficiency, secondary schools are available, and not a few of the young people have either some advanced technical or academic training. But these advantages have not bred snobbery or idleness.

Perhaps Harve's story may be taken as typical. I am condensing it from the original which appeared in Toronto *Saturday Night*:

"Maybe a fellow could build a house if he thought he could. The rich harvest was over, he had had twenty days of threshing with the machine he and his brother owned and a period of comparative leisure was before him. He knew what he wanted; a bungalow, twenty-four by thirty-six feet, with five rooms and a bath.

"He was twenty-seven years old. His formal education had ended with the ninth grade and a couple of terms at the technical school in the city. But his informal schooling had been gleaned by long companionship with farm machinery. He was a natural mechanic. He had taken down and re-assembled engines of all sorts. He had mixed and poured concrete for farm-buildings at home. He could saw boards and drive nails, as every farm-boy must.

"Right! He would build a house, all alone. All he would need would be the materials. Already he had the major part of them; namely, brains, faith, red hair, freckles and a complete set of iron muscles. He wouldn't be able to afford hired labour, but he had a brother and a brother-in-law who gave assurances of help in a pinch. Also he had a good father, mechanically-minded, but crippled by rheumatism, whose brains worked as well as ever and who could answer questions.

"With an old road-scraper hitched to the tractor he made the cellar-excavation and squared it up with pick and shovel. Then he went shopping for cement and lumber—one hundred bags of cement and so many thousand feet of clean spruce and jack-pine, two by six, two by four, two-inch plank and dressed siding. He got a good quantity price at the mills forty miles away and all winter hauled the stuff in his truck. He hauled gravel and sand which cost him nothing. He bought enough

56

second-hand brick for a chimney. He drove a forty-foot well in his cellar. Then at a sale he bought a wrecked gas engine for fifty cents, spent sixty-five cents for some new parts and soon had the revived engine put-putting like a new one. He hitched it to the pump and was ready for action. Between seeding and harvest he made the forms for the foundation, mixed and poured the concrete, put in the cellar window frames, sawed and laid the joists, erected his frame and got the roof on.

"Then he went to see the extra-special girl and took her for a drive to see the house. That drive was extended. They picked up the girl's parents and kept going until they reached a city fifteen hundred miles away. There they got married, with Father and Mother as witnesses, both pledged to secrecy. For the girl worked in a Calgary office which had a stupid rule; that a stenographer who got married was automatically fired. Jessie had an idea that if she could work one more year she could furnish the house.

"The bridegroom went home and resumed his overalls. His brother-in-law was an electrician as well as a farmer and undertook to wire the house in accordance with standard practice, since Harve was promising himself a wind-generator and a double row of storage batteries.

"The building continued, Harve making a model kitchen according to Jessie's specifications; sink and range, shelves and drawers, all in the right places, and the woodwork made radiant with cream enamel. He did the plumbing for sink, bath and basin, cutting and threading the pipe. He did much more. Then the bride came home and an astonished neighbourhood joined in a *charivari* of admiration."

I seem to recognize in Harve and Jessie the same spirit that I knew and loved in the men and women of forty or fifty years ago. I look back on my Alberta days with continual thanksgiving, and if I grow garrulous about them, perhaps I may be excused.

By Way of Appendix

The young and bustling missionary, covering fifty miles or so of prairie every Sunday in four leaps, with a sermon at each landing-spot, passed out of view. We heard from time to time of his appointment to other fields, but it seemed that contact was broken. Then (after forty years) an inquiry of the Victoria College Library brought information that Rev. Frank J. Johnson, B.A., B.D., was a superannuated minister, living in Edmonton. Graciously he consented to dig into his memory for incidents of the happy times. What follows is based on his reply:

"I was within a year of graduation at Victoria College when I volunteered for mission work in Alberta, on the understanding that I could finish my course in Arts and Theology by correspondence while at work on the field. I was appointed by the first Alberta Conference of 1905 to the budding village of Crossfield and to the settlers, present or prospective, in that area. My 'parish' extended about twenty miles from north to south and fifty miles from east to west. I entered happily— and boldly, I'm afraid—on the considerable task of covering a thousand square miles in the saddle, or, where trails existed, by a team and buckboard.

"This region of virgin prairie was being rapidly taken up. Frequently ten or twelve cars of settlers' effects were on the Crossfield sidings awaiting their turn to be unloaded. One of my tasks was to meet the newcomers, find out their location, give them a cheering word and discover their church affiliation— if any. We were all tenderfeet together.

"These new acquaintances were both interesting and inspiring. The atmosphere of optimism prevailed. Everyone felt that he had filed on one of the best quarter-sections in the district, if not in the world, and was full of days of work and ambition to develop it. Few had more than just enough money for the bare necessities of getting located. Others had less and trusted in possible earnings to help them along. All were on a common level and happy in the prospect of new homes.

"In the pastoral visitations following the brief greetings at Crossfield the missionary always was warmly welcomed and had many pleasing surprises. Frequently he asked, 'How did you get so much done in so short a time?' The usual reply was, 'We all helped.' Those were great days of co-operation and honest friendship, each delighting in his neighbour's progress.

"In Crossfield our Sunday congregation soon became too large for the schoolhouse. A church was a necessity, but how could one be built with so little money in sight? Our modest aim was a partially-completed building, a mere shell, to cost not over $1,200. Our assets were faith, homesteaders' zeal and a small grant from the Methodist headquarters. Volunteer work was organized under the direction of a carpenter and a mason. Three miles from the village an outcrop of limestone jutted from the face of a coulée. Under an experienced quarry-man the missionary learned how to blast and dress stone, and in the fall of 1905 our stone foundation was finished.

"The winter was so mild that we could work almost every day, often without a coat or gloves, and at Easter, 1906, we opened and dedicated our new church; not uncompleted, but finished within and without. We had the first plastered interior for miles around. We had raised in cash and pledges over $2,000, covering all obligations; a little here, a little there, and a considerable amount from unexpected quarters; but all from the people of the district.

"Perhaps the wealthiest of all our homesteaders was a retired Great Lakes captain. His wife and daughter attended church regularly, but the captain, not at all. Nevertheless a donation was solicited.

"'I'll give you a fat sow,' said the captain, with a laugh.

"Immediately it was accepted, with a responsive laugh; a cheerful interview on both sides.

"Next morning the preacher and the town butcher drove out to take delivery. The captain was surprised. 'Do you really mean you'll accept that sow?'

"'Surely, and with thanks. Already she has been sold. About what does she weigh?'

"'All right, the joke's on me.' But two or three days later in Crossfield the captain said, 'Look here. I don't want it to get around that all I gave to the church was an old, fat sow. Here's a hundred dollars.' At the church opening he gave another hundred to start a fund for the building of a church shed to shelter the horses.

"The numerous cowboys in the district got interested. Meeting me on the trail the salute would be, 'Hello, there, sky-pilot. How's that church coming on?'

"'Fairly well, considering the shortage of the necessary around here.'

"Then out would come a roll, and sometimes a ten, or even a twenty would be peeled off and transferred, always with the warning, 'But I don't want my name to go down.' These cowboys were rough-and-ready, but kindness and generosity rode the trails with every one of them. Frequently several were in the congregation.

"The Crossfield Church choir was amazing. Fourteen of the twenty members were trained singers. The director had been choirmaster of a large city church in Ontario. The soprano soloist had had church and concert experience. Three sons of a United States minister and one son's wife had been touring American cities as a concert party. The pianist, her two brothers and a sister were talented relations of P. P. Bliss, famous composer of Gospel songs.

"Not only was the church music excellent but the choir concerts which were frequent and good always attracted a full house. Few large churches have music as fine as the Crossfield choir provided. It was a continuing inspiration to the minister.

"Meanwhile over my thousand square miles settlers generously opened their homes for occasional services. I think more particularly of Mr. Jackson, Mr. Thomas and Mr. Richard. Their fidelity and happy fellowship fortified the missionary.

"As schools were established here and there school teachers appeared, mostly young and attractive. But they didn't teach long; some for six months, some for a year. This was a bachelors' country and bachelors go a-courting when opportunity serves. The girls rode in as school teachers, and rode out as brides, causing perpetual distress to school boards who had dreams of permanence in educational affairs.

"Out west of Crossfield the continuing loss of teachers compelled the board to drastic action. They engaged an elderly spinster, and deputed me to take her out on Sunday and introduce her. The news that a new teacher was coming had spread rapidly, and when we reached the school the yard was filled with bachelor settlers and cowboys, all in their best attire, and with saddles and bridles a-gleam with spit-and-polish.

"The grey-haired lady accompanying me was (I heard later) mistaken for my mother, or possibly an aunt. Probably (they thought) the teacher had already arrived and was indoors. I shall never forget the hush of surprise and disappointment when after the service I introduced the teacher. Indeed I had had the greatest difficulty in conducting the service with proper dignity and decorum. When at last I came out of the schoolhouse the trim saddle horses and the gay riders had vanished.

"Those pioneer days of the tenderfoot settlers and the prairie sky-pilot will be a treasured memory while life lasts."